Kyrie Irving

By Jon M. Fishman

AMAZING ATHLETES

Lerner Publications ◆ Minneapolis

Lerner Publications Company
A division of Lerner Publishing Group, Inc.
241 First Avenue North
Minneapolis, MN 55401 USA

For reading levels and more information, look up this title at www.lernerbooks.com.

Library of Congress Cataloging-in-Publication Data

The Cataloging-in-Publication Data for *Kyrie Irving* is on file at the Library of Congress.
ISBN 978-1-5124-1336-6 (lib. bdg.)
ISBN 978-1-5124-1363-2 (pbk.)
ISBN 978-1-5124-1364-9 (EB pdf)

Manufactured in the United States of America
1-39808-21331-4/29/2016

TABLE OF CONTENTS

Kyrie Irving drives toward the basket in a game against the Los Angeles Lakers.

BACK ON TOP

Cleveland Cavaliers **point guard** Kyrie Irving bent his knees and eyed the basket. Players dashed all around him on the court. He jumped and released the ball. *Swish!* The long **jump shot** was good for the first basket of the game. A few seconds later, Kyrie hit another shot to give his team four points.

Kyrie and the Cavs were playing against the Los Angeles Lakers on February 10, 2016. LeBron James of Cleveland and Kobe Bryant of Los Angeles usually lead the way for their teams. James and Bryant are two of the best players in National Basketball Association (NBA) history. But this game belonged to Kyrie.

Kyrie puts up a shot for the Cavaliers near the beginning of the game against the Lakers.

In the first half, the young point guard made shots from all around the court. He nailed long **three-point shots**. He made **layups**. He **rebounded** and passed to teammates for **assists**. At halftime, the Cavs had the lead, 64–47.

Kyrie helps the Cavaliers keep their lead over the Lakers.

Kyrie's knee injury kept him on the sidelines during the first two months of the 2015–2016 NBA season.

Kyrie was finally feeling comfortable on the court. He had missed most of the first two months of the season due to a knee injury. He called the healing process "a long, long road." But by February, he felt healthy and confident again.

Kyrie's favorite food is macaroni and cheese.

Kyrie takes the ball to the basket for two more points.

In the second half of the game against Los Angeles, Kyrie continued to make baskets. As time ticked away, the Lakers couldn't stop him. Instead, they **fouled** him. But the Cleveland point guard calmly made his **free throws**. He ended the game with 35 points. It was the most he'd scored that season. The Cavs won, 120–111.

Like all athletes, Kyrie has had to deal with injuries. But when he's on the court, he's one of the most exciting players in the NBA. In just five seasons in the league, he's already been to All-Star Games and won a most valuable player (MVP) award. Kyrie has a bright future.

Kyrie was born in Melbourne, Australia *(above)*.

YOUNG LORD

Kyrie Andrew Irving was born on March 23, 1992, in Melbourne, Australia. His father, Drederick, played **professional** basketball in Australia at the time.

Kyrie watched Drederick closely when he played basketball. Even when Kyrie was a baby, his eyes followed his father on the court. When he was 13 months old, Kyrie picked up a basketball and dribbled with one hand. His father caught the moment on video. "Wow," Drederick said. "Look at him." About one year later, Kyrie and his family moved to the United States.

Kyrie means "lord" in Greek.

Kyrie *(left)* and his father playing basketball together

When he was four, tragedy struck. Kyrie's mother, Elizabeth, died suddenly after a short illness. The family was shocked. Drederick was left alone to raise Kyrie and his older sister, Asia.

Kyrie posing with his father, Drederick, at their home in West Orange, New Jersey

Drederick moved the family to West Orange, New Jersey. He kept Kyrie and Asia focused on their schoolwork and sports. Kyrie loved basketball. When he was in fourth grade, he wrote "Goal: Play in the NBA" on a piece of paper. He kept the paper for years.

In 2006, Kyrie began high school at Montclair Kimberley Academy in Montclair, New Jersey. He was an instant hit on the basketball team. In two seasons, he became just the second player in school history to score more than 1,000 points. In 2007–2008, Kyrie helped Montclair win the state championship.

The next season, Kyrie switched schools. He enrolled at St. Patrick's High School in Elizabeth, New Jersey. St. Patrick's played against schools that had more students and better basketball teams than Montclair faced.

As a senior at St. Patrick's, Kyrie averaged 24.5 points and 6.5 assists per game. College **scouts** all around the United States were paying attention to the young point guard. He played in all-star games such as the 2010 McDonald's All-American Game. Kyrie had become one of the top-ranked high school players in the United States.

Kyrie scores a basket during the McDonald's All-American Game.

Kyrie began playing basketball for Duke University in 2010.

DUKE

After high school, Kyrie had his choice of schools. Almost any college basketball team would have been glad to add such a highly ranked player. In 2010, he enrolled at Duke University in Durham, North Carolina.

The Duke Blue Devils are one of the most successful college basketball teams in the United States. The season before Kyrie joined the team, they won the **National Collegiate Athletic Association (NCAA) tournament**. Duke's coach, Mike Krzyzewski, is also the coach of the US national team. He has coached NBA superstars such as Carmelo Anthony and LeBron James in the Olympics.

Duke's head coach, Mike Krzyzewski, giving instructions to the Blue Devils during a game

Kyrie was the starting point guard for the first game of Duke's 2010–2011 season. They faced Princeton University. On the first **possession** of the game, Kyrie blocked a shot by the other team. When Princeton had the ball again,

Kyrie dribbles around the defense in a game against Princeton University.

he reached out for a **steal**. Then he ran down the court and sank a shot for Duke's first basket of the season. He finished the game with 17 points and 9 assists.

The big performance against Princeton was a great way for Kyrie to start his college career. He also played well in his next few games. But in a game against Butler University, Kyrie injured his foot. After the game, reporters asked Krzyzewski if Kyrie would be out for the rest of the season. "He could be, he could be," Krzyzewski said.

The Blue Devils have won the NCAA tournament five times: 1991, 1992, 2001, 2010, and 2015.

Kyrie didn't miss the rest of the season, but it took him a long time to return to the court. On March 18, 2011, Duke played Hampton University in the NCAA tournament. Kyrie played for the first time in about three months.

At first, Kyrie was too excited to play well against Hampton. He missed an easy shot.

Then he was called for a foul. "But once I got the butterflies out, I started to play really well," he said. Kyrie finished the game with 14 points. Duke crushed Hampton, 87–45.

Kyrie shoots a basket in his first game after being injured for three months.

Kyrie tries to block a shot in an NCAA tournament game against Michigan.

ONE-AND-DONE

Duke's next opponent in the 2011 NCAA tournament was the University of Michigan. The Michigan Wolverines were a much tougher opponent than Hampton had been. Down by two points in the final seconds of the game, the Wolverines put up a shot. The ball hit the **rim** and bounced away. Kyrie had scored 11 points to help Duke win the game, 73–71.

The Blue Devils lost to the University of Arizona in their next game, 93–77. Kyrie scored 28 points for his best performance of the tournament. But it wasn't enough. "The tournament is cruel . . . when you don't win," said Krzyzewski.

As soon as the game against Arizona was over, Duke fans started wondering about Kyrie's future. Even though he'd missed much of the season, he'd shown that he was one of the top college players in the country. Most scouts thought that if he left college, Kyrie would be one of the first players chosen in the NBA **draft**. But after the game against Arizona, he wasn't ready to declare an end to his college career. "I could definitely see myself wearing a Duke uniform again," Kyrie said. "I don't want to take it off right now."

Sometimes top college athletes play just one season before leaving school for professional sports. Some people call these players one-and-done athletes. Kyrie had enjoyed his time as a Blue Devil. But it was hard to pass up the prospect of earning millions of dollars playing professional basketball. In April 2011, Kyrie decided to leave school to join the NBA. "I love everything about Duke and I'm going to miss it," he said.

On June 23, 2011, the Cleveland Cavaliers chose Kyrie with the first pick in the NBA draft.

Kyrie averaged 17.7 points, 2.3 rebounds, and 2 assists per game in the NCAA tournament.

It was clear that he'd made the right decision by leaving the Blue Devils after just one season. "I'm looking forward to getting to Cleveland," Kyrie said. "I can't wait."

Kyrie shakes hands with NBA boss David Stern after being chosen by the Cleveland Cavaliers in the NBA draft.

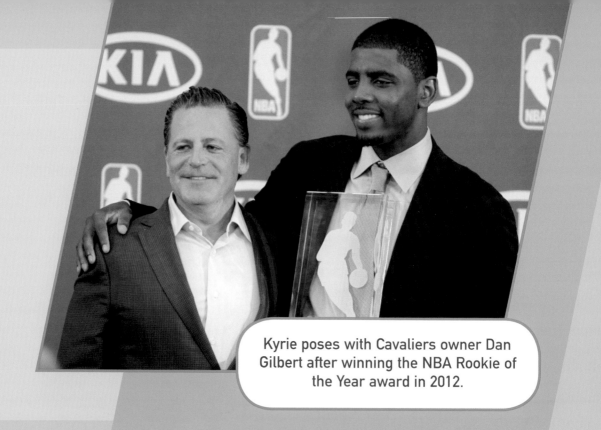

Kyrie poses with Cavaliers owner Dan Gilbert after winning the NBA Rookie of the Year award in 2012.

NBA ROYALTY

Just like in high school and college, Kyrie didn't need time to adjust to his new team. He starred in the NBA right from the beginning. As a **rookie**, he averaged 18.5 points and 5.4 assists per game for the Cavs. He was voted the 2011–2012 NBA Rookie of the Year.

As an NBA superstar, Kyrie had new opportunities to help others. In 2013, he traveled to South Africa with the United Nations Children's Fund (UNICEF). He supported the group's Schools for Africa program. "I saw firsthand how early childhood education and school sports activities are making a difference in these kids' lives," Kyrie said. He also works with groups to help people in need in the Cleveland area.

In 2014, Kyrie was voted to play in the NBA All-Star Game for the second time. He scored 31 points and added 14 assists to help his team win, 163–155. His incredible play earned him the All-Star Game MVP award.

LeBron James is the youngest player to ever win an All-Star Game MVP award. Kyrie is the second-youngest player to win the award.

LeBron James had left the Cavaliers after the 2009–2010 season to join the Miami Heat. But in 2014–2015, he returned to Cleveland. With LeBron and Kyrie leading the way, the Cavs instantly became one of the best teams in the league. They finished the regular season with a record of 53–29. In the **playoffs**, they made it all the way to the NBA Finals.

Kyrie *(left)* dribbles toward the basket in a 2014 game.

Kyrie drives the ball between two Golden State players during the NBA Finals.

The Cavs faced Stephen Curry and the Golden State Warriors in the Finals. Game 1 of the series was close from beginning to end. The game went to **overtime**. With just over two minutes left in overtime, Kyrie dribbled the ball toward the basket. But then he twisted awkwardly and fell to the court. His knee was injured, and he wouldn't play again until the next season. Golden State won the game and the NBA Finals.

Kyrie didn't let the injury or the loss to Golden State get him down. "This is just a setback," he said. With Kyrie's basketball skills and desire to succeed on the court, he may have another chance to win the NBA Finals soon.

Selected Career Highlights

2015–2016 Missed the beginning of the season with a knee injury

2014–2015 Voted to the NBA All-Star Game for the third time
Averaged 21.7 points and 5.2 assists per game with the Cavs

2013–2014 Won the All-Star Game MVP award
Voted to the NBA All-Star Game for the second time
Averaged 20.8 points and 6.1 assists per game with the Cavs

2012–2013 Voted to the NBA All-Star Game for the first time
Averaged 22.5 points and 5.9 assists per game with the Cavs

2011–2012 Voted NBA Rookie of the Year
Averaged 18.5 points and 5.4 assists per game with the Cavs
Chosen with the first overall pick in the NBA draft

2010–2011 Helped Duke win two games in the NCAA tournament
Enrolled at Duke University

2009–2010 Played in the McDonald's All-American Game
Scored 24.5 points, 5 rebounds, and 6.5 assists per game for St. Patrick's

2008–2009 Led St. Patrick's to the state championship
Scored 17 points, 5 rebounds, and 5 assists per game for St. Patrick's

2007–2008 Led Montclair Kimberley to the state championship
Scored 29 points, 10 rebounds, and 7 assists per game for Montclair Kimberley

2006–2007 Scored 15 points, 5 rebounds, and 6 assists per game for Montclair Kimberley

Glossary

assists: passes to teammates that result in scores

draft: a yearly event in which teams take turns choosing new players from a group

fouled: pushed or grabbed to stop from scoring. Fouls may result in free throws.

free throws: unopposed shots from the free throw line

jump shot: an attempt to make a basket in which both feet leave the ground

layups: shots taken with one hand near the basket

National Collegiate Athletic Association (NCAA) tournament: a yearly tournament in which 65 teams compete to decide the national champion

overtime: time added to the end of a game to decide a winner

playoffs: a series of games held to decide a champion

point guard: a player whose main job is usually to set up teammates for baskets with good passes

possession: the time a basketball team has the ball

professional: paid to play a sport

rebounded: gained possession of loose balls

rim: the metal hoop that a basketball net is attached to

rookie: a first-year player

scouts: basketball experts who watch players closely to judge their abilities

steal: take possession of the ball from the other team

three-point shots: attempts to make a basket from behind the three-point line

Further Reading & Websites

Fishman, Jon M. *Stephen Curry*. Minneapolis: Lerner Publications, 2016.

Savage, Jeff. *LeBron James*. Minneapolis: Lerner Publications, 2016.

Savage, Jeff. *Super Basketball Infographics*. Minneapolis: Lerner Publications, 2015.

Cleveland Cavaliers
http://www.nba.com/cavaliers
The official website of the Cavs provides fans with recent news stories, statistics, biographies of players and coaches, and information about games.

NBA Draft
http://www.nba.com/draft
Visit the official site of the NBA draft to find out all about the next NBA superstars.

Sports Illustrated Kids
http://www.sikids.com
The *Sports Illustrated Kids* website covers all sports, including basketball.

Index

Photo Acknowledgments

The images in this book are used with the permission of: © Jason Miller/ Getty Images, pp. 4, 6, 8, 29; Phil Masturzo/Akron Beacon Journal/ Newscom, p. 5; © David Maxwell/Getty Images, p. 7; © iStockphoto.com/ GordonBellPhotography, p. 10; © Denise Truscello/Getty Images, p. 11; © July Xanthos/NY Daily News/Getty Images, p. 12; Jim Rinaldi/Icon SMI/ Newscom, p. 14; AP Photo/Troy Wayrynen, p. 15; © Jonathan Daniel/Getty Images, p. 16; © Peyton Williams/Getty Images, p. 17; AP Photo, p. 19; Chris Keane/Reuters/Newscom, p. 20; AP Photo/Bill Kostroun, p. 23; AP Photo/ Mark Duncan, p. 24; © Christian Petersen/Getty Images, p. 26; AP Photo/Ben Margot, p. 27.

Front cover: Geoff Burke/USA Today Sports/Newscom.

Main body text set in Caecilia LT Std 55 Roman 16/28.
Typeface provided by Adobe Systems.